HAS THE ADJUSTMENT PROCESS WORKED?

HAS THE ADJUSTMENT PROCESS WORKED?

Paul R. Krugman

INSTITUTE FOR INTERNATIONAL ECONOMICS
WASHINGTON, DC
October 1991

Paul R. Krugman is a Visiting Fellow at the Institute for International Economics and Professor of Economics at the Massachusetts Institute of Technology. He has served as Senior International Economist on the staff of the Council of Economic Advisers and is the author of numerous works on international trade and monetary economics, including *The Age of Diminished Expectations: U.S. Economic Policy in the 1990s* (1990) and *Rethinking International Trade* (1990).

INSTITUTE FOR INTERNATIONAL ECONOMICS
11 Dupont Circle, NW
Washington, DC 20036-1207
(202) 328-9000   Telex: 261271 IIE UR   FAX: (202) 328-5432

C. Fred Bergsten, *Director*
Linda Griffin Kean, *Director of Publications*

The Institute for International Economics was created by, and receives substantial support from, the German Marshall Fund of the United States.

Printed in the United States of America   93 92 91   3 2

Library of Congress Cataloging-in-Publication Data

Krugman, Paul R.
    Has the adjustment process worked? / Paul R. Krugman.
        p.   cm.—(Policy analyses in international economics; 34)
    "September 1991."
    Includes bibliographical references.
    ISBN 0-88132-116-8 (pbk.): $12.95
    1. Balance of payments—Congresses.   2. Structural adjustment (Economic policy)—Congresses.   I. Title.   II. Series.
HG3882.K78   1991   91-33990
382'.17—dc20   CIP

382.17
K94h

Contents

6 THE INTERNATIONAL ADJUSTMENT PROCESS: A VERDICT page 45

How the International Adjustment Process Works *page 45*
Implications for International Economic Policy *page 47*

APPENDICES

REFERENCES *page 61*

TABLES

FIGURES

Preface

The large trade imbalances that emerged among the world's major economies in the 1980s have been a focal point of the research program of the Institute since its inception. I began calling attention to the problem in the early 1980s and, with William R. Cline, addressed its most crucial geographical dimension in *The United States–Japan Economic Problem* (1985). Stephen Marris provided a comprehensive analysis that included the financial dimension of the issue in *Deficits and the Dollar: The World Economy at Risk* (1985). Cline reviewed the first phase of the policy response in *United States External Adjustment and the World Economy* (1989), and I drew on Cline's preliminary analyses in my *America in the World Economy: A Strategy for the 1990s* (1988).

On the basis of these studies, I and others at the Institute have participated actively in the national and international debate on the adjustment issue. Hence we have felt a responsibility to continually assess the progress or lack thereof in the realization of our analytical projections and policy prescriptions. The need to reassess became expecially acute in the late 1980s as widespread disappointment emerged over the perpetuation of sizable imbalances despite large changes in exchange rates and a number of policy steps. This study derives from a conference organized by the Institute in late 1990 to analyze the extent to which actual trade shifts had tracked the expectations of both economists and policymakers, and to draw lessons for both from the dramatic swings of this period.

As with several earlier Institute studies, we are releasing the results of this project in two different formats in an effort to meet the needs of different groups of readers. I have edited the full set of papers prepared for the conference (updated through mid-1991) and comment on them in *International Adjustment and Finance: The Lessons of 1985–1990,* to be released shortly. The present essay, which is also the summary final chapter of the larger volume, presents Paul R. Krugman's view of its major analytical conclusions and their policy implications.

The Institute for International Economics is a private nonprofit institution for the study and discussion of international economic policy. Its purpose is to analyze important issues in that area, and to develop and communicate practical new approaches for dealing with them. The Institute is completely nonpartisan.

The Institute was created by a generous commitment of funds from the German Marshall Fund of the United States in 1981 and now receives about 12 percent of its support from that source. In addition, major institutional grants are being received from the Ford Foundation, the William and Flora Hewlett Foundation, the William M. Keck, Jr. Foundation, the Alfred P. Sloan Foundation, the C. V. Starr Foundation, and the United States–Japan Foundation. A number of other foundations and private corporations are contributing to the highly diversified financial resources of the Institute. About 12 percent of those resources in our latest fiscal year were provided by contributors outside the United States, including about 2 percent from Japan. No funding is received from any government.

The Board of Directors bears overall responsibility for the Institute and gives general guidance and approval to its research program— including identification of topics that are likely to become important to international economic policymakers over the medium run (generally, one to three years), and which thus should be addressed by the Institute. The Director, working closely with the staff and outside Advisory Committee, is responsible for the development of particular projects and makes the final decision to publish an individual study.

The Institute hopes that its studies and other activities will contribute to building a stronger foundation for international economic policy around the world. We invite readers of these publications to let us know how they think we can best accomplish this objective.

C. FRED BERGSTEN
Director
October 1991

1 Introduction

The 1984 *Economic Report of the President,* published early that year but drafted in late 1983, correctly forecast that in 1984 the US merchandise trade deficit would for the first time in history exceed $100 billion. It also offered, in advance, a diagnosis of that unprecedented deficit. About $30 billion of the shortfall, the report argued, could be regarded as structural or normal, the counterpart of the US surplus in services. The rise in the deficit above that structural level could be attributed in part to the Third World debt crisis, which slashed US exports to Latin American nations after 1982, and to the relatively strong cyclical performance of the US economy, which had begun to recover from the 1982 recession, generating increased demand for imports. The lion's share of the prospective deficit, however, was explained by the strong dollar, which by late 1983 had risen some 30 percent from its low point (in nominal terms) in 1980. The strong dollar, in turn, could be explained by the collision between the federal budget deficit and a tight monetary policy; together these raised real interest rates in the United States, which in turn attracted foreign capital inflows.

It seems fair to say that the attitude toward international adjustment expressed in that report was shared by most mainstream international economic analysts at the time. It was an attitude of policy concern but analytical confidence: "We know how to cure this deficit," the report seemed to say; "All we need is the political will."

In September 1985, finance ministers from the five leading market economies met at the Plaza Hotel in New York to coordinate a strategy for reducing current account imbalances among the leading industrial nations. Whether because of that meeting or coincidentally, the dollar (which had already begun to decline before the Plaza) fell massively from its 1985 peak and continued falling until early 1988.

The decline of the dollar, however, did not at first produce a corresponding decline in current account imbalances. Indeed, table 1 shows through much of 1987 that these imbalances continued to grow, leading

1

TABLE 1 Current account balances in the G-3 countries, 1985–90

Country	1985	1986	1987	1988	1989	1990
United States						
Billions of dollars	−122.3	−145.4	−162.3	−128.9	−110.0	−97.0
As a percentage of GNP	−3.0	−3.4	−3.6	−2.6	−2.1	−1.8
Germany						
Billions of dollars	16.5	39.7	45.8	50.4	55.4	47.8
As a percentage of GNP	2.6	4.4	4.1	4.2	4.6	2.6
Japan						
Billions of dollars	49.2	85.8	87.0	79.6	57.2	47.5
As a percentage of GNP	3.7	4.4	3.6	2.8	2.0	1.7

n.a. = not available.

Source: Organization for Economic Cooperation and Development, Main Economic Indicators, various issues.

to widespread assertions that the traditional international adjustment process no longer worked. Growing US trade deficits and Japanese surpluses created a political furor, while academic researchers turned their attention to a variety of models designed to show how uncertainty, strategic moves by oligopolistic firms, or other exotic factors might be frustrating trade adjustment.

Now the reconsideration is itself being reconsidered. Since 1987 the US trade deficit and the Japanese and German surpluses have shrunk, especially as measured against GNP. Correspondingly, the political heat has been turned down in the United States, where attention has shifted to other issues, notably foreign direct investment. Yet the questions raised during the initial period of disappointment over the results of the post-Plaza exchange rate realignments remain. Has the adjustment process worked?

As Herbert Stein has pointed out (chapter 6),[1] taken literally this is a meaningless question. It is a fundamental proposition that things that cannot go on, like massive current account deficits, don't. The corollary is that things that must adjust, do. So of course the international adjustment mechanism has worked: we are where we are, and we got here from there.

When one asks whether the international adjustment mechanism has worked, however, what one is really asking is whether it has worked more or less as we thought it would, and whether it has worked in a way that we find acceptable. That is, has the standard view of international adjustment been borne out by experience?

These are not only important questions but opportune ones as well. The 1980s were a difficult time for those who had to make policy, or a living, in the international economy. But the same volatility that whipsawed firms and nations provided a unique opportunity for economists to settle old controversies. From a scientific point of view, if not otherwise, the 1980s were a wonderful decade for the international economy—indeed, Robert Z. Lawrence (1990) argues that in the end

---

1. Chapter references in this study refer to the conference volume *International Adjustment and Finance: The Lessons of 1985—1990,* edited by C. Fred Bergsten (forthcoming in 1991 from the Institute for International Economics.)

we got virtually as good a controlled experiment on the effects of exchange rate changes as if it had been deliberately designed. This was not one of those stretches of history when everything is a smooth trend, all models fit well, and everything is too collinear to allow reliable estimation of anything. The decade's record of huge swings in exchange rates and trade balances gives us the best opportunity ever to sort out competing schools of thought in the economics of international adjustment, and perhaps even to get reasonably solid estimates of some key parameters.

In November 1990 the Institute for International Economics held a conference entitled "Has the International Adjustment Process Worked?" The purpose of the conference was to bring together leading researchers on balance of payments adjustment to discuss and evaluate the lessons of adjustment during the era of dollar decline. This monograph is an effort to pull together the insights gained from that conference.

The study is in five parts. The first part restates what we can regard as the mainstream view of international adjustment. The second part summarizes the three main intellectual challenges to that view that emerged during the period of post-Plaza frustration. The third part discusses the implications of these alternative views of international adjustment for exchange rate policy (and for trade policy as well, since the two turn out to be linked). The fourth part examines the lessons of recent experience in the United States, Japan, and Germany. The final part of the study draws some conclusions.

2 The Mainstream View of International Balance of Payments Adjustment

Most though by no means all international economists on the policy circuit carry in the back of their heads and on the backs of their envelopes a basic model of international adjustment that derives from the model devised by Robert A. Mundell and J. Marcus Fleming in the 1960s, with adjustments for expectations both of depreciation and of inflation. We might call this revised Mundell-Fleming model the "Mass. Ave." model, since its main contemporary adherents in the United States work on or near a Massachusetts Avenue in either Cambridge or Washington.[1] Bergsten (US Congress 1981) had something like this model in mind when he offered an early warning of the trade consequences of the Reagan administration's emerging monetary-fiscal policy mix. A version of this model implicitly underlay Martin Feldstein's original statement (1985) of the "twin deficits" idea—the view that the trade deficit could be viewed as the sister of the budget deficit. More explicitly, essentially this same model underlay the assessment in the 1984 *Economic Report of the President*. Most major econometric models of the world economy, such as the Federal Reserve Board's MCM model and the Japanese Economic Planning Agency model, are also in effect elaborate versions of the model sketched out here.

I begin with a brief summary of the theory, then follow with a summary of the conventional wisdom about the corresponding empirical parameters.

---

1. In Cambridge, the main strongholds of this model are Harvard University, the Massachusetts Institute of Technology, and the National Bureau of Economic Research. In Washington, they include the Brookings Institution, the Institute for International Economics itself, and—a few blocks off Massachusetts Avenue—the staff of the Federal Reserve.

The Mass. Ave. Model

The standard international macroeconomic model can be summarized in terms of a few key relationships (an algebraic statement is provided in appendix A). The first element of the canonical model is the Keynesian view that output is demand-determined at any point in time. Demand for the domestic goods of any individual country is the sum of that country's domestic spending plus net exports. Domestic spending depends at minimum on income and the real interest rate.

Net exports are assumed at minimum to depend on domestic income, foreign income, and the real exchange rate. This equation could easily have additional arguments—wealth and expected future income in demand, expenditure as well as output; in general these do not seem to add much explanatory power in practice, and a simple formulation in which imports and exports have constant elasticities with respect to domestic and foreign income respectively seems to work quite well.[2] It is crucial, however, to allow for lags in the effect of the real exchange rate. Without exception, empirical models of net exports find a substantial lag in the response of trade flows to relative prices. This is not surprising, since decisions by importers to change sources take time, and decisions by potential exporters to seek out new markets and step up production take even more time. At the same time, most empirical models suggest that a currency depreciation is fairly quickly passed through in a rise in import prices. As a result, most models indicate the presence of at least some J-curve, that is, an initially perverse response of the trade balance to the exchange rate change: although the *volume* of imports falls following a devaluation, their *value* (in domestic currency) initially rises because of higher prices, and the gradual rise in exports is initially insufficient to offset this adverse impact on the trade balance.

A third element in the standard model is an ordinary and fairly uncontroversial monetary sector. A supply of money (M) determined by the

---

2. For an exploration of a variety of different specifications, see Helkie and Hooper (1988). Surveys of empirical evidence on trade may be found in Goldstein and Khan (1985) and Bryant et al. (1988a and b).

central bank must equal a demand for money balances that depends on income, the price level, and interest rates.

A fourth element is some kind of exchange rate equation. The typical formulation is something like the following: investors require that expected returns on domestic and foreign interest-earning assets be equal. They also see the real exchange rate as reverting gradually toward some long-run expected rate, say by eliminating a fraction of the gap every year. This implies that the real exchange rate is simply a function of the real interest rate differential: the higher are, say, US real interest rates relative to Japan's, the stronger the dollar.

To finish off the Mass. Ave. model, we need to determine prices. The typical formulation is one in which the price *level* is predetermined at any point in time. The rate of inflation is then determined by some expectations-adjusted Phillips curve in which inflation depends on the level of output relative to trend and on expected or core inflation; core inflation in turn is adaptive, adjusting slowly in response to actual inflation.

This standard formulation is essentially an updated IS-LM model, in which markets for goods are brought into equilibrium with those for money and financial assets. It is a dynamic model, with the dynamics arising from the lag in trade adjustment that results from sluggish export and import responses to relative prices, from the gradual adjustment of prices (from the Phillips curve), and from slow changes in the inflation expectations embodied in the core inflation rate. In discussions of adjustment, however, it is common to abstract from the dynamics, by thinking in terms of a medium run in which trade adjustment to the exchange rate is more or less complete but in which the other lags— the adjustment of prices and inflationary expectations—can be ignored. Whether such a medium run, which is implicitly the time domain of the Mundell-Fleming approach, is a useful shortcut is an empirical question. In estimated models, however, it seems to be.

It is straightforward in this shortcut model to think about the consequences of changes in monetary and fiscal policy for the external balance. Consider first the predicted effects of an expansionary fiscal policy. Such an expansion will raise demand for domestically produced goods and services, leading to an expansion in output. As output rises, however, the demand for money will also rise, pulling up the interest rate. This will lead to crowding out of private investment; in addition, the rise in domestic relative to foreign interest rates will produce a currency appreciation that leads to a fall in net exports at any given level of output. Thus, fiscal expansion leads to both an expansion of output and an exchange rate appreciation—and to a decline in net exports for both reasons.

Next consider the predicted effects of an expansionary monetary policy. The initial effect will be to lower the interest rate; this lower rate will stimulate investment and, since the domestic interest rate has fallen relative to foreign rates, lead to currency depreciation. Currency depreciation will in turn stimulate net exports at any given level of output, providing a second channel of expansion. The overall effect is a rise in output accompanied by a decline in the currency, with an ambiguous effect on the current account.

One could imagine combining a contractionary fiscal policy with an expansionary monetary policy just large enough to leave income unchanged. This would produce currency depreciation at a constant level of income. It is also possible to imagine a change in the exchange rate unconnected to any macroeconomic policy change.[3] Suppose, for example, that for some reason the long-run expected exchange rate falls—perhaps because of jawboning by G-7 ministers. The effect will be a downward shift in the exchange rate associated with any given domestic interest rate. Since this will have a stimulative effect on net exports, there will also be an expansion in the economy. This expansion will drive up interest rates, reducing but not eliminating both the depreciation and the increase in net exports resulting from changes in expectations.

Empirical Conventional Wisdom

The Mass. Ave. model is not purely a matter of pencil-and-paper speculation. On the contrary, a large body of econometric work has attempted to fit elaborated versions of this basic model to real-life data, and to

---

3. Which is not to say that one can imagine the exchange rate changing for no reason at all: *something*, if only a change in expectations, has to change to move the exchange rate. Opponents of the Mass. Ave. view sometimes accuse proponents of treating the exchange rate as if it were not a determined as well as a determining variable; this charge is unfair.

TABLE   2   **Representative elasticity estimates**[a]

	Imports	Exports
Median income elasticity	1.8	1.2
Median long-run price elasticity	1.1	0.8
Median mean lag from exchange rate change to initial trade volume response (years)	0.6	0.8
Median exchange rate effect on price	0.9	0.2

a. Figures are median estimates of six independent econometric models surveyed in Bryant et al. (1988) and the estimates of Lawrence (1990).

Sources: Bryant, Ralph C., Gerald Holtham, and Peter Hooper, eds. 1988b. *External Deficits and the Dollar: The Pit and the Pendulum.* Washington: Brookings Institution; Lawrence, Robert Z. 1990. "US Current Account Adjustment: An Appraisal." *Brookings Papers on Economic Activity* 2:343–82.

estimate policy multipliers. The relationships among output, exchange rates, and net exports in particular have been the subject of a vast empirical literature.

Table 2 offers some summary results aimed at giving a more or less standard view of the responses of imports and exports to income and exchange rate changes. It presents median estimates for US trade from seven trade models: six that were part of a model comparison conducted by Bryant et al. (1988), together with the recent work of Lawrence (1990).

The first line of table 2 presents estimated income elasticities for imports and exports. The main point to note here is that in general estimates for the United States find a higher income elasticity of import than of export demand, so that if US and rest-of-world output were to grow at similar rates, the US would need a persistent depreciation of the dollar in order not to have a steadily widening trade deficit. This observation plays a key role in one of the challenges to the standard view, what I call the "secularist" view, discussed below.

The second line of the table presents median price elasticity estimates for imports and exports. Basically, such estimates hover in the vicinity of one; this is large enough to ensure that a real depreciation will in fact

TABLE   3   **Estimated median response of the US current account to a 20 percent real depreciation of the dollar** (percentages of GNP)[a]

Year	Change in current account
1	−0.21
2	0.51
3	1.32
4	1.43
5	1.45

a. Figures are the median values of six independent econometric models.

Source: Bryant, Ralph C., Gerald Holtham, and Peter Hooper, eds. 1988b. *External Deficits and the Dollar: the Pit and the Pendulum.* Washington: Brookings Institution.

increase net exports, but still much smaller than many economists might have assumed a priori.

The standard view also attributes substantial lags to the response of trade flows to relative price changes, as illustrated in the third line. The 7- to 10-month mean lag of trade *volumes* behind prices translates, as will be documented in a moment, into a substantially longer lag of trade *values* behind the exchange rate.

Finally, as the last line of the table shows, conventional estimates also strongly suggest that a dollar depreciation is reflected in a decline in the US terms of trade, albeit somewhat less than one-for-one. A depreciation of the dollar leads to some rise in US dollar export prices, but for the most part US exporters pass their lower costs measured in foreign currency on to their customers; similarly, while foreign exporters to the United States absorb some of the rise in their dollar costs, most of the rise is passed on to US consumers.

Table 2 by itself does not give a full picture of the conventional dynamics of the response of the trade balance to depreciation. Both because many models imply some lag in the response of trade prices to the exchange rate, and because the standard view implies that initial increases in real net exports will be largely offset by valuation effects, the improvement in the nominal trade balance following a depreciation takes much longer than the mean lags in table 2. Fortunately, Bryant et al. offer a table of simulated responses of the current account to a 20 percent dollar depreciation. Table 3 presents median values (unfortunately omitting the more recent Lawrence estimates). The important point here is that, by the conventional wisdom, it takes more than two years for the bulk of the response of the current account to currency changes to take place.

The Conventional Wisdom and the Adjustment Debate

I have taken some space to describe this more or less standard model for three reasons. The first is that this model represents the underlying text for much discussion of international adjustment, but it is often a hidden text, because economists are unwilling either to be excessively formal (if they are speaking to policymakers) or so brazenly ad hoc (if they are speaking to their colleagues).[4] This leads to much confusion. Even in conferences where speakers and audience are professional international economists, there are obvious moments when half the participants are listening to music that eludes the rest.

A second reason to restate the basic model is to clear the air of some common accusations leveled against international economists who focus on the role of the exchange rate. In particular, economists who ask how the exchange rate affects trade are often accused of a partial-equilibrium viewpoint—of failing to understand basic accounting identities or missing the point that whatever changes the exchange rate will also change other things. But the Mass. Ave. model does in fact respect the basic identities: the equation that sets output equal to aggregate demand can also be rewritten $S - I = NX$, or $NX = Y - A$ (where S is aggregate saving, I is investment, NX is net exports, Y is income, and A is domestic absorption). And the model is clear in allowing factors other than exchange rate changes to affect the trade balance. A fiscal

---

4. The Mass. Ave. model may not seem all that ad hoc to the lay public. In academic macroeconomics, however, it has become increasingly *de rigueur* to base all discussion on models with rigorous microeconomic foundations, and the criteria for what constitutes rigor have gradually narrowed to the point where virtually all policy-oriented macroeconomic analysis has become unacceptable in polite academic company.

expansion raises output as well as the real exchange rate; a monetary expansion, although it leads to real depreciation, has an ambiguous effect on net exports in principle (and little net effect in practice, according to the empirical studies surveyed by Frankel 1988). When mainstream international economists discuss international adjustment, implicitly they are discussing a scenario in which there is simultaneous contractionary fiscal policy and offsetting monetary expansion, which leaves output roughly unchanged while depreciating the currency.

The main reason for setting out a standard view, however, is as a vantage point from which to survey alternative views. The main alternative views can be summarized by contrasting them with what the mainstream view asserts about the need for dollar depreciation. In the mainstream view:

- A policy mix such as fiscal contraction *cum* monetary expansion that drives down the dollar in real terms without a large economic expansion will be *successful* in reducing the US external deficit;
- The real depreciation associated with such a policy mix is *necessary* in order to achieve that deficit reduction, or at least to achieve it without undesirable side effects such as recession;
- The extent of depreciation needed is more or less *predictable*, because there is a stable relationship between trade flows and real exchange rates.

The three main alternative views, all of which emerged in some form during the IIE conference, each deny one of these three assertions. The next part of this study examines each of their cases in turn.

3   Challenges to the Mainstream View

Is currency depreciation effective at raising net exports, or does it simply offer a fire sale of US assets to foreign investors? Is depreciation necessary, or is it irrelevant to an adjustment process driven by saving-investment balances? Is the appropriate exchange rate predictable, or are we chasing a moving (and receding) target as US competitive decline requires an ever-lower dollar? Amid the widespread dismay over the initial failure of the post-Plaza exchange rate adjustments to narrow trade imbalances, influential voices argued that exchange rate adjustment either did not work, was not necessary, or was an inadequate response to deeper competitive issues. For reasons that will become clear shortly, I will refer to the proponents of these three views as structuralists, shmooists, and secularists, respectively.

Do Exchange Rates Work? The Structuralist View

A generation ago, it was common for economists from developing countries, especially in Latin America, to argue that for a variety of reasons the price mechanism in general and currency devaluation in particular did not work well in their countries. For example, they argued that there were institutional rigidities: a quasi-feudal agricultural sector would not expand production even if offered higher prices; organized urban workers would demand higher wages to offset the inflationary impact of a devaluation. They further argued that their countries' reliance on exports of primary products, which faced inelastic demand, meant that any attempt to increase export volumes would drive down the price received without increasing the foreign exchange earned. And they argued that the lack of domestic production competing with imports would prevent any fall in imports as a result of devaluation. Thus, they asserted, devaluation would not succeed at improving the trade balance, but would simply lower real incomes and/or lead to an acceleration of the rate of inflation.

This so-called structuralist view is now out of fashion among development economists, but it sometimes reappears in different contexts. During the 1970s, a form of structuralism achieved considerable policy prominence in the United Kingdom, where it was strongly pushed by the Cambridge Economic Policy Group (see, for example, Godley 1979 and other references discussed below). In the United States, a sort of neostructuralism emerged in 1986–87 amid the widespread disappointment over the continuing rise in the US trade deficit in spite of a sharply falling dollar.

Some of this revival of structuralism represented a crude failure to appreciate the role that relative prices play in economic decisions; for example, it was common for lay commentators to deny that a lower dollar would reduce US purchases of Japanese goods, asserting either that the United States produced no competing goods or that the quality of the Japanese products was so much better that no conceivable price differential would make any difference.

Politically motivated structuralism also gives foreign barriers to trade an exaggerated role as an explanation of persistent US trade problems: it was common in the mid–1980s to hear assertions that foreign protectionism would prevent any substantial increase in US exports. Proponents of a "get tough" policy with Japan, including Fallows (1989), Prestowitz (1989), and Dornbusch (1989), still in effect assert that, in the case of Japan, implicit import restrictions are blocking trade adjustment.

More interestingly, however, during the 1980s a sophisticated version of neostructuralism emerged, which held not that relative prices were unimportant, but that the strategies of imperfectly competitive firms, especially in the face of uncertainty about future exchange rates, might frustrate the adjustment process.

The two most important concepts in this new literature were those of "pricing to market" and "hysteresis." Pricing to market occurs when firms, rather than pass on exchange rate changes into export prices, try to hold onto their market position by keeping prices in the importing country's currency stable. Such behavior was obvious in some consumer goods during the 1980s, especially when "gray markets" began to develop in some Japanese products reimported into Japan. A possible theoretical basis for pricing to market was suggested in an influential paper by Dornbusch (1987), and the extent to which it occurs in practice was documented more fully in several elegant empirical papers by Marston (1989, 1990) using Japanese data. Two key questions remain, however: Was pricing to market more widespread and severe in the 1980s than in the past? And did it in any important way frustrate the adjustment process?

Pricing to market is, in the light of Marston's work, undeniably something that really happens. More controversial is the idea of hysteresis: that markets lost when a country's currency rises in value may not be regained when the currency declines to its original level. This might occur if one thinks of market share as a kind of investment, achieved through costly creation of consumer reputation and of distribution networks. Once foreign firms have exploited a high dollar to establish new markets in the United States, they may hold onto them even at a less favorable exchange rate; once US firms have decided to abandon foreign markets for the same reason, they may not find it worthwhile to try to break back in even if the dollar falls to its original level.[1] Initially introduced as a hypothesis in Baldwin and Krugman (1989), the idea of hysteresis gained popularity as trade imbalances persisted, but despite efforts by Baldwin (1988) it has never really been firmly established as an important phenomenon.

In general, the empirical force of arguments suggesting that exchange rates are ineffective at correcting current account imbalances has fallen considerably since 1987. We will consider individual-country experiences in the next section, but by any measure the period since 1987 has seen a marked narrowing of deficits and surpluses, especially relative to growing world income (with the counterpart developments in the United States, Japan, and Germany of course dominating the picture).

It is also becoming embarrassingly clear that at least some of the apparently anomalous behavior of trade volumes and prices in the 1980s represents oddities in the data, rather than in reality. Lawrence (1990), in particular, has shown that if computers are excluded, the behavior

---

1. Richard Baldwin has suggested the term "beachhead effect" for this phenomenon, with an implied military analogy. For example, it was a lot harder to get Saddam Hussein out of Kuwait than it would have been to stop him from getting in in the first place.

of US trade in the 1980s looks more or less in line with pre–1980 expectations. Measurement of trade in computers is notoriously subject to difficulties: given the rapid improvement in technology, it is extremely difficult to establish reliable indices of either prices or volumes. The Bureau of Economic Analysis, the US Commerce Department agency that monitors US economic performance, attempts to adjust statistics on computers to represent the improvement in quality. Lawrence's evidence suggests that they have overcorrected, or at least that behavior in the computer market is wholly unrepresentative of behavior elsewhere.

This does not mean that the structuralist critique is completely groundless. There are at least two kinds of mild structuralism that remain reasonable sources of concern.

First, while crude structuralism is often characterized by misplaced concreteness ("America doesn't make VCRs—and can you imagine the Japanese buying Chevys?") that misses the complexity and flexibility of real economies, some degree of concreteness is not out of place. As Allen J. Lenz's paper for the IIE conference (chapter 2) reminds us, aggregate trade performance is the sum of trade performance in individual industries. While there is a great deal of commonality in industry experiences, there are also individual industry stories that matter. Telling the story of the subsidized rise of Airbus as a competitor to US aircraft exports, or of Detroit's competitive failures, is no substitute for macroeconomic analysis, but neither is it irrelevant.

Second, even if one believes that the effectiveness of the exchange rate in the long run has been vindicated, we nevertheless live in the short run. And one need not be a strong-form structuralist, believing in the complete ineffectiveness of exchange rates to alter trade balances, to share some short-run structuralist concerns. A weak-form structuralist would argue that at least in the very short run, and possibly for a little longer, the real exchange rate changes needed to achieve substantial trade adjustment are simply too large to be tolerable. Suppose, for example, that a country with a large trade deficit were suddenly to be deprived of foreign funding, and was thus compelled to reduce its trade deficit rapidly. If it tried to do so purely via depreciation, it would subject its economy to a severe inflationary shock. As a result, the adjustment process for countries in balance of payments crisis typically involves economic contraction as well as depreciation.

This is, of course, the celebrated "hard landing" scenario of Stephen Marris (1987). Despite Marris's warnings, such a hard landing never materialized in the United States. One should not conclude from this that hard landings are impossible—ask the Latin Americans.

Why, then, was the United States able to avoid one? Marris's paper for the IIE conference (chapter 6) suggests that the main reason lies in the forbearance of capital markets, which did not insist on a sudden reduction of the US trade deficit, but were instead willing to continue financing the United States through a prolonged process of gradual adjustment. As argued in appendix B, this patience of the financial markets was actually something that one should have expected, although Marris argues that it was aided to a significant degree by the cooperative guidance of policymakers. With occasional official intervention averting any free-fall in the dollar, the United States was able to continue to attract financing during the long wait before depreciation could bring the trade deficit down, and was therefore not forced into the devaluation-stagflation cycle that has produced hard landings in Latin America and elsewhere.

We will discuss country experiences below. To anticipate the conclusions, however, we can say that on the whole recent analysis has tended to confirm the old-fashioned view that exchange rates work. There are clearly significant lags, as there always were, and as a result every major exchange rate change will be followed by a period of agonizing over whether the change will eventually prove effective. There are some suggestions that the lags may be longer than we realized. With hindsight, however, we can see that reports of the demise of the exchange rate mechanism in the 1980s were premature.

Are Exchange Rate Changes Necessary?
The Shmooist View

During the 1960s there was a bitter dispute between leftist economists in Cambridge, England (led by Joan Robinson and Nicholas Kaldor), and moderate economists in Cambridge, Massachusetts (led by Robert M. Solow), over the meaning and nature of capital. For reasons that remain slightly puzzling, the English Cantabridgians believed that the idea that a meaningful aggregate measure of capital existed was a crucial ideological prop for capitalist exploitation; anti-Solow modelers therefore ridiculed the MIT school of capital theory for its working assumption that economies produce a single homogeneous good usable either for capital or for consumption. Somewhere along the line, commentators took to referring to this all-purpose good as a "shmoo," after a cartoon creature (invented by Al Capp) that would obligingly turn into whatever food one wanted.

Shmoo-theoretic models are common in international monetary economics; it is often useful in thinking about monetary and financial issues to abstract from relative price changes by imagining a world in which all countries simply produce a single good. In such a world, changes in national saving-investment balances would translate directly into changes in trade balances, without the need for any accommodating adjustments in relative prices or output. (John Williamson [chapter 5] felicitously described this during the IIE conference as an "immaculate transfer.")

A shmooist would argue that this simplification is actually a reasonable description of trade adjustment in the real world. Of course, nobody thinks that we live in a one-good world; the question is whether trade adjustment can be accomplished without significant real depreciation on the part of the deficit countries. That is, the shmooist denies that real exchange rate changes are a necessary or a helpful part of the adjustment process.

This position is essentially that taken by Bertil Ohlin in his debate with John Maynard Keynes over the transfer problem (see Mundell 1989 for an account of this classic debate). If one country sends money to another—whether as a gift (or tribute) or to finance investment—the counterpart must be a trade surplus on the part of the donor, and a deficit on the part of the recipient. Correspondingly, narrowing or eliminating these imbalances is like ending a transfer. Keynes argued that, in order to generate the required trade surplus, a donor country would have to experience a real depreciation; Ohlin's position was that the transfer itself could generate the required trade surplus, without the need for price changes.

In its original version, Ohlin's position was based on the point that a donor country, by spending less, automatically reduces its demand for imports, while a recipient, by spending more, automatically increases its demand for the donor's exports. If the two countries have the same spending pattern at the margin, this will lead to exactly the right trade surplus, with no need for any price change.   257045

Obviously this is not what the conventional wisdom asserts. The basis of the conventional wisdom was clarified by Dornbusch, Fischer, and Samuelson (1977): it rests essentially on the imperfect integration of markets for goods and services. Because many (most) goods and services are nontraded, most of a marginal dollar of spending in any large country goes to purchase domestic goods. As a result, there is a presumption that a reduction in, say, the flow of Japanese funds to the United States will reduce the demand for US goods and raise the demand for Japanese goods; this will require a rise in the relative price of Japanese goods, which is to say a real appreciation of the yen.

The leading contemporary defenders of the Ohlin-shmoo position are Robert Mundell and Ronald I. McKinnon; at the IIE conference (chapter 5), Mundell presented a wide-ranging essay on the history of thinking about the international adjustment mechanism, focusing largely though not exclusively on this question. Both Mundell and McKinnon have pointed out that the attempt to justify conventional presumptions about the effects of a transfer by appealing to the importance of nontraded goods is contingent on one's views about the structure of production—specifically the view that exports and nontraded goods are better substitutes in production than nontraded and import-competing goods. It is possible in principle to imagine a world in which much of output is nontraded, yet in which a transfer can take place with no change in relative prices—or even a real depreciation in the recipient country.

Again, we will turn to country evidence in the next section. To anticipate, however, we may argue that the apparent success of income-and-elasticity trade equations for the US and Japanese trade balances, as documented at the IIE conference in papers by William R. Cline and Masaru Yoshitomi (chapters 2 and 3), provides the empirical basis for asserting that while Keynes may have been wrong in theory, he was right in practice. The conference also, however, addressed a third case, that of Germany. As a paper by Norbert Walter showed (chapter 4), Germany's current balance with its Western European neighbors has showed highly variable surpluses, under a regime of more or less fixed nominal exchange rates, and little obvious correlation between trade flows and real exchange rate indices. Others have observed the same thing, and they use the European experience under the European Monetary System to suggest that a fixed exchange rate system can in fact easily accommodate necessary balance of payments adjustments.

A key question is therefore whether the apparent contrast between the experiences of Germany, on the one hand, and the United States and Japan, on the other, undermines the conventional wisdom that exchange rate changes are a necessary part of the adjustment mechanism.

Is the Equilibrium Exchange Rate Stable? The Secularist View

Ask noneconomists about the causes of the US trade deficit, and they are unlikely to mention the exchange rate. Instead, they will view the deficit as a symptom of a broader decline in "competitiveness"—in productivity, technological leadership, and product quality. Economists may dismiss this lay view, secure in their knowledge that $X - M$ always equals $S - I$, even if the X's are shoddy and the M's superb. The popular view does, however, point up a practical problem with the standard view of exchange rates, namely, the problem of secular change, of a shift over time in the trade balance associated with any given real exchange rate.

Let me label as "secularists" those who believe that the relationship between exchange rates and trade is unstable. Laypeople—for example, policy-minded engineers at MIT—are often both secularists and structuralists. That is, they see trade imbalances as the result of shifting technological advantage between countries, and they do not believe that exchange rate adjustment can offset such shifts. Few economists are such strong-form secularists. Weaker versions of the position, however, do emerge on several issues.

The most widely held secularist position among economists is the assertion that there is a consistent downward trend in the equilibrium real dollar, that the US currency needs to depreciate a little bit each year in order to keep the trade balance in the same place. The prime evidence for this is the observation that by most measures the real dollar ended the 1980s about where it began, yet the United States went from rough balance in its current account to a persistent large deficit. In his paper for the IIE conference, Cline calls this the Krugman-Lawrence paradox; it is a more recent version of the observation by Houthakker and Magee (1969) that the United States appears to face a foreign income elasticity of demand for its exports that is lower than its own income elasticity of import demand. That is, if income grows at the same rate in the United States and in the rest of the world, US imports will tend to grow more rapidly than US exports; thus, even at a constant real exchange rate, the US trade deficit will tend to rise, and over the long run a steady real depreciation of the dollar will be necessary in order to avoid an ever-growing trade deficit. Japan's experience offers a counterpart paradox: the yen ended the decade far stronger than it entered it, without any move into deficit.

Considerable effort has been devoted to explaining the apparent secular downward trend in the dollar. To secularists the answer seems obvious: it is the statistical counterpart of the decline in US "competitiveness," i.e., the declining relative quality and technological sophistication of US goods. Cline suggests, on the contrary, that it may be a statistical illusion, which goes away if one uses the right price index, but this view was not favorably received by most others at the IIE conference. Peter Hooper (chapter 2), who has long argued for the inclusion of supply-side variables (such as measures of productive capacity) in trade equations, argues that when this is done the paradox goes away, or even emerges on the other side: US trade performance has been *better* than we might have expected. Some support for Hooper's argument that US competitiveness has actually improved comes from the Japanese experience, where there was an unexpectedly rapid decline in the surplus in 1989–90.

The important point about this argument is that although there are some meaningful disputes among economists about the long-term trajectory of the dollar, in general they are pretty close in their views—at least as compared with lay views about competitiveness. There is general if not universal agreement that there has been a downward trend in the real dollar consistent with trade balance, at least by the usual measures, with the outstanding questions being why and whether that trend will continue. But there is also general agreement that the trend is fairly slow, on the order of 2 percent or less annually. This can amount to a lot over the course of a decade, but it does not make the short- and medium-run response of trade to the exchange rate either unpredictable or irrelevant. In short, most of us may be secularists, but of a very mild form.

We have now described the conventional wisdom with regard to the international adjustment mechanism and the main challenges to that conventional wisdom. We will turn shortly to the experiences of the three largest market economies, to see what light they shed on the process. First, however, we need to ask how the analysis of the international adjustment mechanism affects one's view of appropriate international economic policy.

4 Policy Implications of Alternative Views

The Mass. Ave. View

The conventional analytical wisdom about the role of the exchange rate in trade adjustment is generally associated with a conventional policy wisdom as well. The main purpose of this study is to discuss whether and how the adjustment mechanism works, rather than how it should be used; nonetheless it is important to place this discussion in a policy context.

The essence of the conventional wisdom about adjustment policy was expressed clearly in a classic paper by Harry Johnson (1958). Johnson argued that in order to adjust its trade account—say, to reduce a current account deficit—a country needs to pursue both "expenditure-reducing" policies, such as fiscal tightening, and "expenditure-switching" policies, such as devaluation. Expenditure switching without expenditure reduction would lead to inflation, but reduction without switching would lead to recession. Johnson then went on to assert that normally exchange rate adjustment would be an effective expenditure-switching policy.

Johnson's analysis, or something like it, underlies two basic mainstream propositions about international economic policy:

- The trade balance is a macroeconomic issue: Trade deficits fundamentally reflect a disparity between spending and income, not a market failure. They are therefore not an appropriate subject for trade policy instruments such as tariffs and import quotas: a trade deficit can be dealt with by a combination of domestic expenditure reduction and depreciation, and trade policy should be based solely on microeconomic considerations.
- Exchange rate flexibility is a valuable policy tool: The ability to change the exchange rate makes it much easier to deal with payments imbal-

23

ances, and this piece of the adjustment mechanism should not be given up—for example by establishing immutably fixed exchange rates—lightly.

If we follow the implications of these propositions, we are led to a view of international economic policy that is basically an international extension of conventional wisdom about the relationship between macroeconomic and microeconomic policy. Since the 1950s most US policy economists (if not always most academic macroeconomic theorists) have believed that the government should take an active role in macroeconomic stabilization but otherwise leave markets mostly to themselves. In this conventional view of economic policy, macroeconomic tools—monetary and perhaps fiscal policy—should be used to maintain an appropriate level of aggregate demand. With the problem of aggregate demand allocated to macroeconomic policy, microeconomic policies can then be formulated on pure efficiency grounds; in general this means that an activist macroeconomics is combined with free-market microeconomics.

In the international extension, one adds to the problem of aggregate demand the problem of payments imbalances. This problem can, however, be solved either through deliberate adjustment of the exchange rate or through adoption of a regime of floating exchange rates in which payments problems do not limit a country's freedom to follow expansionary monetary policies. With flexible exchange rates, in turn, there is no need for other instruments to deal with payments problems; this leaves one free to advocate free trade. So one arrives at the same basic recommendation: activism on the macro side, but laissez-faire on the micro side.

Critics of the conventional wisdom on macroeconomics, naturally enough, attack this point of view from both left and right. Interventionists think that job creation should be pursued through microeconomic as well as macroeconomic means, for example through regional and industrial policies; monetarists and their even more free-market-oriented successors think that the government should be as laissez-faire about aggregate demand as it is about supply and demand in individual markets.[1]

---

1. These two kinds of challenge to conventional wisdom have each had a peculiarly limited area of success in the United States. Government intervention to save particular jobs often wins out over the arguments of economists in practice, for example in the Chrysler bailout, but has virtually no intellectual respectability. Opposition to an active stabilization policy, usually based on equilibrium models of the business cycle, is wide-

Structuralists and shmooists are, in effect, the international equivalents of leftist and rightist critics of the conventional wisdom on domestic monetary policy, challenging the two basic policy propositions from opposite directions. Let us consider each in turn.

The Structuralist Case for Protection

Structuralists argue that exchange rates do not work as an adjustment mechanism, or at any rate work only at an unacceptable cost. Thus something else is needed. The "something else" is at best an industrial policy, at worst simple protectionism.

The argument may be schematically illustrated by a picture like figure 1. In that figure, the curve represents the relationship between the exchange rate and the trade balance as a structuralist might perceive it. Even structuralists generally agree that at some sufficiently low dollar the United States could balance its trade—if nothing else, at a very low dollar sheer lack of purchasing power would curb US demand for imports. What a structuralist like Robert Kuttner believes, however, is that the United States is currently at a point where modest dollar depreciation has only a small or even a perverse effect on the trade deficit, as represented by point 1 in the figure. Getting the deficit down substantially, say to the level at point 2, would require a very large fall in the dollar; this would in turn imply large costs in the form of worsened terms of trade and domestic inflationary pressures. As Kuttner puts it (1991, 108), "the danger is that a cheaper dollar will only make the United States a poorer country, without making its products fully competitive."

It would therefore be greatly preferable to shift the entire curve up through some other means. Kuttner and other contemporary American structuralists are slightly evasive about what they propose, although skepticism about the effectiveness of exchange rates is generally followed in their writings by favorable discussions of managed trade. A nicely explicit discussion, however, was offered some years ago by the

---

spread and perhaps on its way to being dominant in academic economics, but has had virtually no impact on policy

FIGURE 1   The structuralist view of the exchange rate–trade balance
relationship

Trade balance

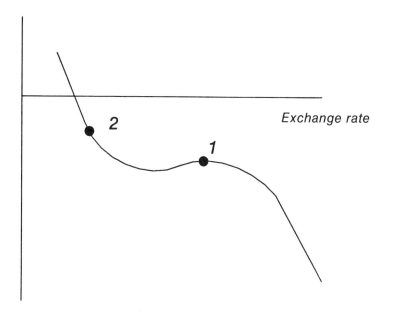

Cambridge Economic Policy Group (CEPG; Cripps and Godley 1976, 1978; Fetherston and Godley 1978; Godley 1979). The CEPG view was that UK growth was being constrained by the need to avoid running large current account deficits; that devaluation was ineffective as a way of reducing the deficits, both because of low elasticities and because of resistance by British workers to reductions in their real wages; and that tariffs or import quotas would therefore offer a superior alternative.

An extreme example may suggest the logic of such protectionist leanings. Imagine that at the current exchange rate a country faces a zero price elasticity of demand for its exports, and that its demand for imports is price-inelastic. Then depreciation would actually worsen the nominal trade balance, because while the volume of imports would fall, their value would actually rise. A tariff on imports, however, *would* improve the trade balance, because imports would fall but the price paid to foreigners would not increase.

The key to this example, of course, is that the country is assumed to have substantial market power in trade. In other words, the structuralist argument for protection is really a variant of the optimum tariff argument, which argues that large countries can use tariffs to improve their terms of trade. The economic case for an optimum tariff, however, has nothing to do with balance of payments adjustment: if the United States can successfully raise its welfare by imposing tariffs, there is no strictly economic reason to limit this policy to times when it has a trade deficit.

As a political matter, however, the structuralist case for protectionism may have something to it. There is not much question that large countries like the United States could in fact raise their welfare by imposing fairly substantial tariffs *if the rest of the world did not retaliate*. Indeed, quantitative models of trade like the "computable general equilibrium" model of Whalley (1985) suggest that the US optimum tariff rate is well above current levels, probably above 50 percent. An unprovoked US move to increase tariffs would, however, be seen as a beggar-thy-neighbor policy and would lead to retaliation or at least emulation. Protection undertaken to limit an intractable trade deficit, by contrast, might be much more readily accepted. Indeed, the existing rules of the international trade game embodied in the General Agreement on Tariffs and Trade make explicit allowance for special trade measures to deal with balance of payments problems.

The structuralist view of the adjustment process, then, gives at least indirect comfort to the idea of trade restrictions as a balance of payments tool.

The Shmooist Case for Fixed Exchange Rates

The essential moral of the shmooist view of the adjustment process, if that view is correct, is that exchange rate flexibility is of no value, and hence that the micro-monetary advantages of fixed exchange rates need not be weighed against macroeconomic disadvantages. In other words, the shmooist analytical view of the adjustment process is closely connected with the renewed popularity of fixed exchange rates as a policy recommendation.

The idea that there is a trade-off between the microeconomic advantages of fixed rates and the macroeconomic advantages of floating was first advanced in a classic paper by Ronald McKinnon (1963), in which he presented what has since become the standard theory of optimum currency areas. According to the McKinnon approach, flexible exchange rates are useful because they allow countries to adjust their balance of payments with minimal change in the domestic price level—implying in particular that deficit countries are spared the necessity of deflation and the associated unemployment. On the other hand, exchange rate fluctuations impair the liquidity of domestic money. For a fairly closed economy, the liquidity cost will be small and the benefit of not having to let the balance of payments dictate macroeconomic policy large; the more open the economy, the less valuable is monetary independence and the more costly the degradation that exchange rate instability imposes on the moneyness of money.

This analysis has been taken to imply that the appropriate structure of the international monetary system is one of regional currency blocs, with interbloc exchange rates flexible. Imagine a world composed of very small monetary areas. Since these areas would be very open, they would benefit from being combined for monetary purposes into somewhat larger blocs. If one then imagines grouping successively larger blocs into fixed exchange rate areas, however, one eventually arrives at a point at which the costs of further enlarging the blocs exceed the benefits; at that point, the world will have been organized into optimum currency areas.

Of course, the theory by itself gives no quantitative sense of the size of optimum currency areas. At one extreme, one might make the politically outrageous but by no means economically absurd suggestion that each major metropolitan area would be best served by having an independent currency. At the other, one might argue that while in principle the benefits of ever-larger currency blocs are at some point outweighed by their costs, in practice the world as a whole is an optimal currency area—i.e., that global fixed rates are the best system. At the moment there is widespread support for the idea that optimum currency areas are continent-sized—say, just about as big as the European Community. This is not an unreasonable guess, but it is a belief supported by essentially no evidence.

What the shmooist position on the adjustment mechanism does, however, is to deny that the whole optimum currency argument has any validity. If adjustment does not require changes in the real exchange rate, then there is no value to having nominal exchange rate flexibility as a way of facilitating real exchange rate changes. This leaves only the microeconomic benefits of fixed rates; the optimum currency area is as big as possible.

The foremost proponent of this view is, remarkably, the same Ronald McKinnon who is responsible for the optimum currency area argument. McKinnon (1984), in arguing against the need for exchange rate flexibility, has asserted that real exchange rate adjustment is necessary only for an "insular" economy with less than full mobility of capital—with mobile capital, changes in the saving-investment balance would be automatically converted into changes in current account balances. In some of their writings, McKinnon and others have seemed to suggest that this irrelevance of the real exchange rate is independent of the nature of world markets for goods and services; thus McKinnon wrote that *"With smoothly functioning capital markets, little or no change in the 'real' exchange rate is necessary to transfer saving from one country to another."* (McKinnon 1984, 14, italics in the original). As pointed out above, however, the shmooist view in fact does hinge crucially on how goods and services markets work. In particular, if conventional trade equations are right, then 1980s McKinnon is wrong.

This is not to say that 1960s McKinnon's belief in the benefits of fixed rates may not be right, and that even though exchange rate flexibility is valuable it is not valuable enough to justify flexible exchange rates for the United Kingdom or even the United States. The point is, however, that the shmooist view would make the case for fixed rates a closed one, where conventional wisdom leaves it very much open.

Policy Implications of Secularism

The secularist challenge to conventional wisdom about international adjustment is less directly relevant to policy than the other two. In principle it should perhaps have no exchange rate policy implications at all. Suppose, for example, that I am convinced that there is a secular downward trend in the equilibrium real dollar of 2 percent per year, directly as a result of declining relative US technology and quality, or indirectly as a result of poor US education, deteriorating infrastructure, or whatever. If I hold to conventional wisdom I will declare this to be a microeconomic problem, to be addressed with microeconomic instruments, such as education reform and increased government investment spending. Meanwhile, we should let the dollar depreciate. A shmooist (although he might have trouble accepting the idea that real exchange rates can show any trend) would prefer to allow the nominal dollar to remain stable, and would want the real exchange rate adjustment to take place via relative deflation. In either case, however, conceding the existence of a secular trend need not alter the policy conclusion.

In practice, however, secularism and structuralism are usually associated, and evidence of US secular loss of competitiveness is usually a key part of the arguments of advocates of an aggressive trade policy (such as Clyde Prestowitz's Economic Strategy Institute).

The logic of this association can perhaps best be appreciated by considering the typical dialogue between a mainstream economist and a group of opinionated laymen concerned about US competitiveness (like the belligerent engineers mentioned above). The laymen point to US trade deficits as evidence both that the United States has a major problem of competitiveness and that a direct response in the areas of trade and industrial policy is needed. The economist argues that the trade deficit is a macroeconomic problem, which can be fixed by dollar depreciation. When, as usually happens, the laymen express skepticism about the importance of exchange rates, the economist points to the role of a strong dollar in creating deficits in the 1980s. And at that point the laymen deny that the dollar was the cause of the trade deficit, pointing to US technological and quality failures instead.

As mentioned earlier, Kuttner (1991) is perhaps the clearest published example of how structuralism and secularism can reinforce one another. Arguing against relying on dollar depreciation to solve the trade deficit—and, implicitly, for managed trade as the alternative—he writes that:

> Even with a much cheaper dollar, the factors that have allowed America's competitors to adjust in the past to a cheapening dollar will continue to

operate—the decline in input prices, the ability to outsource, to price to market, and the fact that some products just aren't made in the United States. To a few economists who emphasize structural factors, the danger is that an ever-cheaper dollar will only make the United States a poorer country, without making its products fully competitive. Even at 100 yen to the dollar, how many American-made Chevrolets will be sold in Japan and how many VCRs will be made in the U.S.A.? (Kuttner 1991, 108).

Secularism, then, need not have any particular policy moral. In practice, however, it generally reinforces the structuralist bias toward using trade policy for balance of payments adjustment. And thus even though it perhaps should not, evidence that secular change is modest in extent is in effect a result that supports the case for free trade.

We have now presented the conventional wisdom on the international adjustment process, described the main challenges to that conventional wisdom, and discussed the policy implications of those challenges. The next step is to ask what the experience of the 1980s tells us about how the international adjustment process really works.

5 The Record of Adjustment: 1985–90

The United States

The aggregate story of US external adjustment is simple and familiar, and is shown in figure 2. During the 1980s, the real exchange rate of the dollar went up the hill and came back down. The US current account deficit also went up, lagging behind the dollar. It too came tumbling after, but not all of the way.

Shown a picture like figure 2, neither economists nor the general public are likely to feel the kind of frustration over the United States' failure to adjust that they did three years ago. Nonetheless, US performance raises two major questions.

First, why did the adjustment take so long, with the US deficit continuing to rise for two years after the dollar began to fall? It was suggested above that the empirical consensus is for at least a two-year lag before the bulk of the impact of the exchange rate on the trade balance is felt, but this is not the same as saying that two years should pass before there is *any* impact. The question of the sluggishness of adjustment is connected with the structuralist challenge to conventional wisdom: such sluggishness is *prima facie* evidence for the presence of structural impediments to adjustment.

Second, since the dollar at the end of the 1980s was at about its level at the beginning of the decade, and had been fluctuating around that level for three years, why was the United States still running a substantial current account deficit? This question is, of course, associated with the secularist challenge.

At the IIE conference, William Cline addressed the behavior of US trade from an aggregate perspective. He found that a conventional set of equations actually accounted quite well for the data—there was, in retrospect, no anomaly to be explained. This is similar to the findings

FIGURE 2   United States: real exchange rates and current account deficits, 1980–90

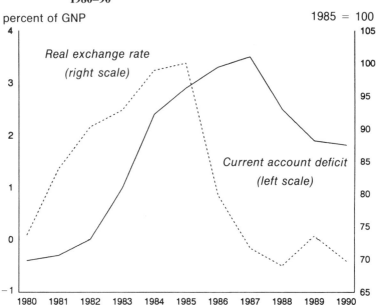

Sources. International Monetary Fund, *International Financial Statistics,* various issues; Organization for Economic Cooperation and Development, *Main Economic Indicators,* various issues.

of Lawrence (1990); hence it is useful to consider the two papers in tandem.

The first point to consider is why the US trade deficit continued to widen for so long before turning down. The Cline-Lawrence answer is essentially that the United States did not carry out the textbook experiment of devaluing its currency from an initial equilibrium position, while holding all else equal. Instead, the dollar's decline followed a period of rise, and it took place against the background of continuing economic recovery. This stretched out the turnaround of the US current account, for two main reasons. First, not all the direct effects of previous dollar rise had worked their way through to trade volumes, so that some continuing rise in the deficit was in effect in the pipeline. Second, because of the previous rise in the dollar, by 1985 US imports greatly exceeded US exports; this created a "gap factor," in which the growth in imports with economic recovery tended to raise the deficit unless offset by a significantly *faster* rate of increase in exports. To take an extreme numerical example, if imports are 500 and exports 200, and if imports are rising by 10 percent per year, then exports must grow by 25 percent just to keep the deficit from growing. These essentially commonplace factors, Cline's analysis suggests, delayed the turn-around in the US deficit by a few quarters relative to what the textbook case might have led us to expect.

The interesting question in that case is why analysts were so willing to call their own conventional wisdom into question. A major part of the answer is probably that official statistics showed what appeared to be very anomalous price behavior, particularly on the import side. Figure 3 makes the point. One line shows the ratio of the US import price deflator to the US GNP deflator, as reported in the national income accounts. Relative import prices fell as the dollar rose, as one might expect; but according to this measure they were very slow to rise as the dollar fell. This observation suggested to many economists—myself included—that something nonstandard was going on, with foreign (especially Japanese) firms showing a new strategic determination to hold onto the markets they had won in the first half of the 1980s.

It has become increasingly clear that the anomaly may have been more in the data than in the real world. Lawrence (1990) has shown that essentially all of the peculiarity in price behavior is associated with computers—and the creation of adequate price indices for computers, as noted above, is notoriously difficult. This point is also made in figure 3, which shows the contrast between the national income accounts measure of relative import prices and Lawrence's constructed index of nonoil, noncomputer relative import prices. Lawrence's measure behaves exactly the way the most conventionally minded economist would expect.

No one has ever claimed that conventional trade equations are highly precise, likely to track the behavior of the trade balance perfectly when projected out of sample. The important question for policy analysis is whether the predictions of such conventional equations are inside the

FIGURE 3   **United States: relative import prices, 1980–90**

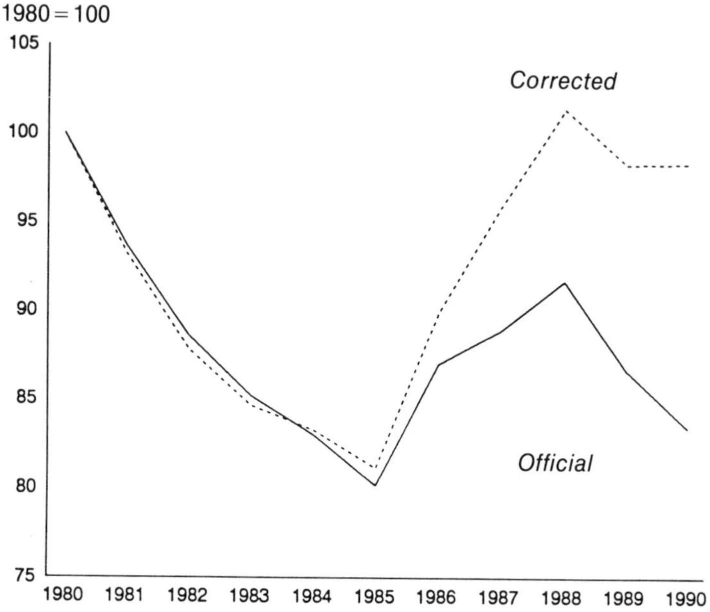

Source: Lawrence, Robert Z. 1990. "US Current Account Adjustment: An Appraisal."
Brookings Papers on Economic Activity 2:343–82.

ballpark, or whether the anomalies are so great that conventional wisdom about the international adjustment process needs to be put aside. The fairly clear answer for the United States at this point is that the conventional wisdom has performed acceptably well, indeed better than we might have expected.

Japan

Japan's adjustment experience during the 1980s was not simply a mirror image of the US experience, but it follows a similar outline. As figure 4 shows, for several years after the 1985 Plaza meeting, Japan's effort at

FIGURE 4 Japan: real exchange rates and current account surpluses, 1980–90

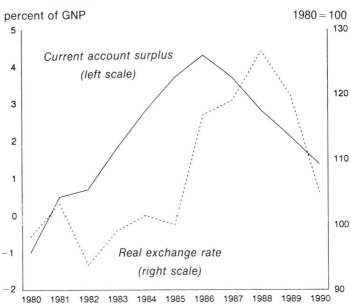

Sources: International Monetary Fund, *International Financial Statistics*, various issues; Organization for Economic Cooperation and Development, *Main Economic Indicators*, various issues.

adjustment appeared to be a failure; then rapid adjustment seemed to occur, raising new questions about whether some more structural change was occurring.

Conventional models of Japanese trade, like the Economic Planning Agency model, find price elasticities of exports and imports comparable to those found for typical models of US trade: fairly low, but easily large enough to satisfy the Marshall-Lerner condition after an initial period of J-curve. At first glance, the behavior of Japan's current account from 1985 to 1988 seems flatly to refute any model predicting that exchange rate changes would produce international adjustment. From its trough in the first quarter of 1985, the yen nearly doubled in

TABLE   4   **Japan: current account, 1985–89** (percentages of GNP)

	1985	1986	1987	1988	1989
At current prices					
Exports of goods and services	16.4	13.1	12.7	13.0	14.6
Imports of goods and services	12.6	8.7	8.9	10.0	12.4
Current account balance	3.8	4.4	3.8	2.9	2.1
At 1985 prices					
Exports of goods and services	16.4	15.2	15.0	15.6	17.1
Imports of goods and services	12.4	12.5	13.0	14.8	17.3
Current account balance	4.0	2.7	2.0	0.8	−0.1

Sources: Organization for Economic Cooperation and Development, *Main Economic Indicators*, various issues; International Monetary Fund, *International Financial Statistics*, various issues.

value against the dollar. Yet Japan's current account surplus in dollar terms was actually higher in 1988 than in 1985, and only slightly below its 1986 peak. Not too unreasonably, this apparent lack of adjustment provoked both political outrage and analytical soul-searching.

In retrospect, however, the stickiness of the Japanese surplus can be explained without much stretching as a consequence of a set of special factors. Masaru Yoshitomi's paper on Japan, like Cline's paper on the United States, shows that ordinary models worked better than many people imagined. The key point is that the stability of the nominal surplus masks a sharp change in real trade flows. As table 4 shows, in volume terms Japanese net exports fell sharply relative to GNP, while imports rose. In constant prices, the current account surplus fell by almost 4 percent of GNP.

This large real adjustment was, however, hidden by price changes. First, the 1985 worldwide collapse in the price of oil, a major import with inelastic demand, inflated Japan's nominal trade surplus. Second, the high initial ratio of exports to imports meant that the perverse valuation effect of a stronger yen via higher dollar export prices was unusually large, leading to an unusually large and prolonged J-curve. Also, as in the case of the United States, the fact that the yen was falling before it began rising, combined with the gap factor, helped to delay adjustment. Overall, the adjustment was not much different from what conventional models would have predicted.

After 1988, there was a reverse puzzle. Although the yen was stable or even rising in real terms after 1988, the Japanese current account surplus fell sharply. This raised speculation that some fundamental structural change had occurred or was occurring, perhaps tied to Japan's surging direct investment abroad: it was widely suggested that Japanese firms, like US firms a generation before, were shifting to overseas production for the Japanese market and local production for foreign markets. If this were the case, it would contribute both to raising Japanese imports and reducing Japanese exports.

Yoshitomi's paper suggests, rather prosaically, that the bulk of the explanation for the current account adjustment lies in more mundane factors. Most of the surge in imports is accounted for by increases in special categories, notably nonmonetary gold and oil, rather than ordinary manufactured goods. The export slump is tied more closely to the developing recession in Japan's export markets than to any large-scale shift of production overseas. The rapid adjustment after 1988, like the sluggish adjustment before it, seems to tell us more about the importance of getting the details right than about any fundamental need to revise our analytical framework.

In addition to the puzzles of overall adjustment, Japanese experience poses three specific questions. First is the question of export pricing. Pricing to market is a well-documented fact for Japanese exports. But was it more widespread in the post–1985 period than previously? The answer seems to be yes, but not dramatically so. Historical relationships between the exchange rate and Japanese export prices would have led us to expect the yen's doubling in value to be accompanied by about a 40 percent fall in yen export prices. In fact they fell about 60 percent. Much of the difference, however, can be attributed (once again) to special factors, notably the crash in oil and other commodity prices. Some residual is left unexplained, but on balance Japanese pricing behavior is not too different from what one might have expected. Yoshitomi argues that any anomalies in Japanese export pricing behavior were too small to explain the apparent anomalies in US import pricing behavior; this view is consistent with the evidence that those US anomalies represent data problems as much as real events.

A second question concerns the macroeconomics of Japan's adjustment. Whereas Japan's move into current account surplus was associated with a tightening of fiscal policy, the unwinding of that surplus was not accompanied by any comparable loosening. How was this possible? The accounting answer is a remarkable surge in domestic private investment demand. The reasons for that surge, however, remain an open question.

Finally, Japan presents its own version of the Houthakker-Magee-Krugman-Lawrence effect. Just as the dollar rose, then fell back to its original level, but left a seemingly permanently higher trade deficit, so too Japan's current account surplus surged and then fell back to more or less its original level, but at a far higher real yen. Again, this apparent secular trend shows up in a difference in income elasticities of exports and imports (a very large difference given Japan's high rate of growth compared with its trading partners); presumably it reflects deeper supply-side phenomena that our models do not capture properly.

Overall, Japan's experience, like that of the United States, appears in retrospect to be far more in line with the standard view of international adjustment than initial reports suggested.

Germany

The Japanese and US adjustment experiences since 1985 have, in a rough sense, been counterparts. Germany, by contrast, has marched to a quite different drummer. While the mark rose against the dollar in tandem with the yen, Germany's current account surplus did not decline: in dollar terms it more than tripled from 1985 to 1989, and (as figure 5 shows) it rose from 2.6 percent to 4.6 percent of German GNP.

Does the German experience contradict the conventional wisdom on trade adjustment? It is not possible to offer as detailed an accounting for German trade as for that of the United States and Japan; for reasons to be discussed in a moment, it is more difficult to estimate German trade equations. Nonetheless, we can say for Germany as for the other two nations that the seeming contradiction of conventional wisdom is more apparent than real.

FIGURE 5 Germany: real exchange rates and current account surpluses

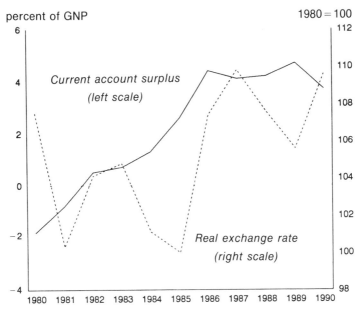

Sources: International Monetary Fund, *International Financial Statistics,* various issues; Organization for Economic Cooperation and Development, *Main Economic Indicators,* various issues.

To some extent the failure of German surpluses to fall, like that of Japan, can be attributed to the fall in oil and other commodity prices. Germany is almost as dependent on imported raw materials as Japan, and in volume terms its imports grew consistently faster than its exports even as its nominal surplus was growing.

The main special feature of Germany, however, is that it is a very open economy, most of whose trade is focused on nearby European nations rather than on the United States and Japan. Indeed, the German trade surplus with the United States declined modestly in dollar terms and sharply in mark terms from 1985 to 1989, while the deficit with Japan widened. These movements were offset, however, by a surging surplus in German trade with the rest of Europe. (The effects of this surplus on the overall dollar surplus were, in yet another valuation story, exaggerated by the overall appreciation of European currencies against the dollar.)

Where the apparent nonadjustment of US and Japanese trade balances has provided ammunition for structuralist critics of orthodoxy, the apparent ease of trade adjustment within Europe provides the strongest empirical case for a shmooist view. As Norbert Walter's paper shows, Germany's current balance with its Western European neighbors has showed highly variable surpluses, under a regime of more or less fixed nominal exchange rates and little obvious correlation between trade flows and real exchange rate indices. Others have observed the same thing—and they use the European experience under the EMS to suggest that a fixed exchange rate system can in fact easily accommodate necessary balance of payments adjustments.

One should, however, be cautious in interpreting the evidence. After one starts to clean up the story by looking at the details, the German balance of payments experience begins to look less exotic.

First, as already mentioned, German trade with non-European nations, especially the United States, has in fact shown the kind of correlation with the real exchange rate that one would expect from the US and Japanese experiences—that is, if there is any evidence for a shmoo world, it ends in Europe.

Second, even the increase in Germany's surpluses with the rest of Europe can be explained in part by currency movements: the deutsche mark depreciated in real terms throughout most of this period.

Third, differences in short-term growth rates explain much of what happens in intra-European trade balances. Precisely because trade among European nations is so large, seemingly small differences in growth rates between countries can have a large effect on trade measured as a share of GNP. One way to put this is the following: since trade is three times as large a share of national income in Germany as it is in the United States, essentially because of intra-European trade, we would expect a difference in growth rates between Germany and its (mainly European) trading partners to have three times the impact on Germany's current account as a percentage of GNP. And in fact during 1985–89 German growth lagged that of other European countries: growth in domestic demand was more than a percentage point slower.

Finally, it is not too surprising that it is difficult to find a clear relationship between real exchange rates and trade flows within Europe, even if one is an unrepentant Mass. Ave. thinker. The reason is that when trade flows are as large as they are within Europe, the exchange rate changes needed to accommodate capital flows are small and easily obscured by growth effects, measurement error, and secular change.

This last point may need some enlarging. Consider a country whose saving rate rises, causing it to begin exporting capital at the rate of 2 percent of GNP. Suppose also that, as many estimates suggest, the price elasticities of both exports and imports are around 1. If the country starts with exports and imports of around 10 percent of GNP (as in the case of the United States), the currency will have to depreciate in real terms by a quite palpable 20 percent. If, however, the country starts like Germany with exports and imports of 30 percent of GNP, the required depreciation will be less than 7 percent. Now, our indices of real exchange rates are not perfect; movements in relative price indices may reflect not only actual changes but also differences in weighting schemes, in quality adjustments, and so on. Also, nobody thinks that equilibrium real exchange rates are constant. So the association between current account shifts and real exchange rate changes, obvious in US data, could easily be masked in German data by a variety of kinds of noise.

Also, while it may be difficult to establish any consistent relationship between real exchange rates and intra-European trade flows, the problems caused by German unification suggest that even Europe is far from being a shmoo economy. The cost of German unification has in effect forced West Germany into a Reaganesque fiscal expansion, which like the Reagan expansion is being offset by a tight monetary policy. Given German dominance of the EMS, the rest of Europe is in effect forced to emulate German monetary contraction. Under a shmooist view, this policy mix would not produce any conflict of interest: the fiscal expansion would offer a common European stimulus, so the same degree of monetary contraction would be appropriate everywhere. The only effect of the German fiscal expansion would be a reduction of Germany's current account surplus—Williamson's immaculate transfer at work.

In fact, however, matters are not working at all smoothly. The lion's share of spending in East Germany falls on West German products, so that a monetary policy tight enough to curb a German boom has produced a recession in the rest of Europe. This demonstrates both that German goods are less than perfect substitutes for those of other European nations, and that there is significant home bias in spending—precisely the combination of factors under which real exchange rate changes are a necessary part of the adjustment process.

Summary

As late as 1988, the trade experiences of the three largest market economies seemed to show that conventional wisdom about the international adjustment process was badly in need of revision. US deficits and Japanese surpluses were stubbornly persistent despite massive exchange rate adjustment, while German surpluses were growing in the teeth of a soaring mark.

The overall impression one gains from studying these experiences more closely is the extent to which apparently anomalous behavior is the result of special factors and annoying details. In all cases the peculiarity of the starting point distorted events. The dollar had been rising before it fell, and on the eve of the dollar's depreciation the United States had a massive trade deficit. The first fact meant that trade imbalances still had momentum behind them; the second that the sheer logic of growth and inflation (a.k.a. the "gap factor") tended to push nominal imbalances up. The worldwide collapse in oil prices affected Germany and Japan more than it did the United States. Differential growth in Europe widened German local surpluses even as the surplus with the United States dwindled.

Peculiar price behavior, the subject of intense interest and speculation, looks less peculiar in retrospect: some of it was illusory, the result of bad indices, and much of the rest was the result of falling raw materials prices.

Even the rather sudden collapse of the German and Japanese surpluses in 1990 seems to have rather pedestrian economic (if not political) explanations. In particular, the suggestion that Japanese direct investment abroad has produced a fundamental change in Japanese trade patterns appears premature at best.

6 The International Adjustment Process: A Verdict

How the International Adjustment Process Works

The 1980s were a time of spectacular gyrations in the international economy. The deepest recession since the 1930s, the rise and fall of the dollar, the debt crisis, and the emergence of current account imbalances on a scale not seen since the 1920s amounted to a testing to destruction of our pet theories of international macroeconomics and finance.

Have the lessons of that experience invalidated traditional views of the international adjustment process? The surprising answer seems to be that they have not. Indeed, on the whole the standard view, what I have called the Mass. Ave. model, holds up remarkably well. In particular, my reading of the papers and discussion from the IIE conference is that, where the problem is one of reducing severe international trade imbalances:

- Exchange rate changes work;
- They are necessary;
- The relationship between trade and exchange rates is stable.

EXCHANGE RATE CHANGES WORK

Before the 1980s, most economists concerned with the empirical modeling of US trade flows made use of simple equations that explained imports and exports by income and relative prices; the income elasticities in these equations tended to be about 2 (a little less for exports, a little more for imports), the price elasticities low in the short run but rising to 1 or a little more after two years or so.

During the 1980s, and in particular as the US trade deficit continued to widen after 1985, it was widely argued that this standard approach was misleading, because strategic behavior by foreign firms in general and Japanese firms in particular meant that exchange rates no longer worked to reduce imbalances. Yet two years after the dollar began its decline, the United States experienced an export boom; this happened just about when and in the magnitude that the traditional models would have predicted. There will always be some analysts who will assert that what works in practice does not work in theory. For the impure-minded, however, the evidence seems overwhelming that exchange rate changes do indeed work.

REAL EXCHANGE RATE CHANGES ARE NECESSARY

During the 1980s a number of economists, most prominently Robert Mundell and Ronald McKinnon, questioned the need for real exchange rate changes as part of the adjustment process. It took a while before it was clear how the two RMs differed from the standard view, but eventually it emerged that their position was essentially a replay of Bertil Ohlin's side of the classic debate over the transfer problem— which has nothing to do either with monetary issues or with the integration of capital markets. And the question they raise is an empirical one: are world markets for goods and services sufficiently well integrated, or with sufficient substitution in demand and supply, so as to allow transfers to be effected with minor changes in relative prices?

As I read the evidence, the answer is a clear no for trade among the United States, Japan, and Europe. Within Europe a better case can be made for immaculate transfers that do not require real exchange rate changes, but even there the problems caused by German unification show that the inability to adjust exchange rates imposes some real costs.

THE RELATIONSHIP BETWEEN TRADE
AND EXCHANGE RATES IS STABLE

Some of the most spectacular changes of the 1980s were of a kind that macroeconomic models are poorly equipped to capture. US leadership in technology and productivity was visibly eroded, while Japan surged ahead. The spread of microelectronics revolutionized a number of industries. Europe first seemed to sink into Eurosclerosis, then shook off its lethargy and boldly drove toward economic unity. One would not have been surprised to find that trade flows, stirred by all these changes, would be very poorly tracked by conventional equations.

The big surprise, then, is that there have been so few surprises. To a man from Mars or from the electrical engineering department, it is the apparent stability of the relationship between exchange rates, incomes, and trade flows, not the drift and errors in that relationship, that would surely seem most remarkable.

The general verdict, then, must be that the international adjustment process has worked, in both meaningful senses: that is, it has worked acceptably, and it has worked about the way conventional wisdom thought it would.

Implications for International Economic Policy

The evidence on the international adjustment process essentially confirms conventional wisdom. That conventional wisdom, however, has been so much under attack of late that to reaffirm it is almost a radical act. Not surprisingly, the policy implications of that reaffirmation similarly confirm an embattled conventional wisdom, one that has perhaps been under even greater attack.

As pointed out earlier, the conventional wisdom on economic policy for open economies is an internationalized version of mainstream thinking on the respective roles of macroeconomic and microeconomic policy at the domestic level. Mainstream economists in general, taking their cue in the first instance from Paul A. Samuelson, have for decades advocated a combination of more or less laissez-faire microeconomic policy with an active use of monetary policy to manage the macroeconomy. These policies, though they may seem contradictory from an ideological point of view, are regarded by the mainstream economist as complements: because the use of monetary policy to control recession and inflation removes any need to use microeconomic policies to pursue macroeconomic goals, it frees the government to focus these policies on allocative efficiency instead.

Challenges to this mainstream point of view come from both the left and the right. Critics from the left would have the government intervene directly in markets to try to improve macroeconomic performance—for example, by using incomes policies to hold down inflation while pursuing expansionary monetary policies, or by using regional policies to try to generate jobs in high-unemployment areas. On the other side, monetarists and their successors would have the central bank forgo any active attempt to stabilize the economy, either because they regard the potential for error as greater than the potential benefits (the traditional monetarist view) or because they regard monetary policy as ineffective (the equilibrium business cycle view).

The policy debate in international economics runs along similar lines. Mainstream international economists—Richard N. Cooper (1971) provides a particularly clear example—have long advocated a combination of free trade and flexible (although not necessarily freely floating) exchange rates. Again, these policies are seen as complementary: exchange rate flexibility means that balance of payments problems are no longer an excuse for protectionism.

The two main challenges to the conventional wisdom about the adjustment process, those of the structuralists and the shmooists, lead directly to (and are largely motivated by) challenges to this policy position. Structuralists argue that exchange rate flexibility is ineffective, because exchange rate changes do not work; this assertion provides the basis for advocating import controls or other forms of managed trade to deal with payments imbalances. Shmooists argue that exchange rate changes serve no useful purpose, and they therefore assert that the benefits of a return to fixed exchange rates are not offset by any costs.

The evidence of the period from 1985 to 1990 allows us simply to dismiss the structuralist concern. Exchange rate adjustment did and does work. Because of the substantial lags in adjustment, all major exchange rate adjustments are followed by a period of confusion and doubt about the adjustment mechanism.[1] In the end, however, the

---

1. For example, similar doubts were voiced following the 1967 devaluation of sterling and the 1971–73 depreciation of the dollar.

depreciation of the dollar and the appreciation of the yen have had just about the effects that conventional wisdom would have predicted. There are intellectually defensible arguments for managed trade, and there are better arguments for domestic industrial policy; the assertion that exchange rates cannot solve payments imbalances is not one of them.

The only possible situation in which a balance of payments argument for import controls might be made is in the context of foreign-exchange crises like those faced by developing countries in 1982–83. Given the evident lags in the response of trade flows to exchange rates, we are all structuralists in the very short run. If a country is faced with an abrupt cutoff of capital inflows, one can therefore argue with some justification for supplementing currency depreciation with temporary import controls. Thus, if Marris's hard landing had in fact materialized in the United States, one could have made a reasonable case for supplementing currency depreciation with temporary import controls.

In fact, however, nothing of the sort happened in the United States. International capital markets proved quite willing to continue to finance the US current account deficit while the effects of dollar depreciation worked their way through the pipeline. One may be a pessimist about the effectiveness of the adjustment mechanism in the short run, but it works in the medium run, and financing has in fact been available to bridge the short-run difficulties. (The relationship between financing and adjustment in the United States since 1985 has puzzled many observers. An effort to provide a stylized description is provided in appendix B.)

While some politicians and a few economic heretics used the slowness of adjustment in the 1980s to argue for managed trade, the main challenge to conventional policy wisdom came from the other direction. During the 1980s there was growing disillusionment with floating exchange rates, and there were many calls for reestablishment of a fixed rate regime or at least for limits on the degree of permissible flexibility. These calls were based in large part on the perception that foreign-exchange markets had performed badly, leading to excessive and costly fluctuations and misalignments. The surprising success of the European Monetary System at stabilizing exchange rates also helped fuel the perception that fixed exchange rates are a more workable system than previously thought. An important part of the case for fixing exchange rates, however, has been the argument that flexible exchange rates do not perform a useful function—that exchange rate changes are not a necessary part of the adjustment mechanism.

What we have seen, however, is that experience since 1985 reconfirms the crucial role of real exchange rate changes in adjustment, and the facilitating role of nominal appreciation or depreciation in achieving such real changes. In other words, the conventional case in favor of exchange rate flexibility is as valid as ever.

Notice that this does not mean that freely floating exchange rates are necessarily appropriate. As pointed out earlier, even conventional wisdom, as embodied in the theory of optimal currency areas, agrees that there is a trade-off between the macroeconomic advantages of flexible rates and the microeconomic advantages of fixed rates. It is still possible to argue that the terms of this trade-off are such as to make a return to fixed rates desirable, or to invoke other factors, such as the need for inflation-prone countries to establish credibility by pegging their currencies. It is also possible to argue for systems of managed exchange rates, for example one based on target zones à la Williamson (1985). The shmooist position, however, is not that the costs of exchange rate flexibility exceed its benefits, but that there are no benefits at all; this is simply not a sustainable view.

What we have thus come to realize, after a decade in which the confidence of economists in the conventional wisdom—and of the public in economists—was profoundly shaken, is that the conventional wisdom was sounder than it seemed. The international adjustment mechanism does indeed seem to work more or less as understood a decade ago, and the policy views that were based on that understanding are still tenable.

This verdict does not deny that there are puzzles, or that much further research is needed. We are not, however, confronted with any great mystery—except, perhaps, the question of why not only the public but so many economists were so quick to declare the adjustment process a failure.

Appendix A

A Formal Statement of the Mass. Ave. Model

The text verbally described the standard model of open-economy macroeconomics, which I have called the "Mass. Ave." model. This appendix offers a brief formal presentation in five equations.

The first equation of this model is the income identity. Income (which is determined by demand in this demand-side model) is the sum of domestic spending, which depends on income and the real interest rate, and net exports, which depend on domestic and foreign income as well as the real exchange rate:

$$y = A(y, i - \pi) + NX(y, y^*, R)$$

The second equation sets money supply equal to money demand, which depends on income and interest rates:

$$\frac{M}{P} = L(y, i)$$

The third equation determines the exchange rate. The typical formulation sets expected returns on domestic and foreign interest-earning assets equal, with expected depreciation equal to the expected inflation differential plus some reversion of the real exchange rate to an expected long-run level:

$$i = i^* + \pi - \pi^* + \theta(R^e - R)$$

Price determination completes the model. The rate of inflation is determined by an expectations-adjusted Phillips curve:

$$\frac{\dot{P}}{P} = g(y) + \pi$$

FIGURE A.1 **Determination of the real exchange rate in the Mass. Ave. model**

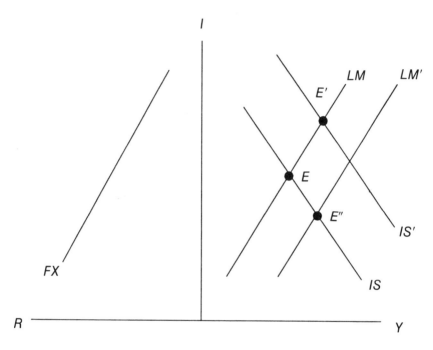

Finally, expectations of inflation are adaptive, adjusting slowly toward actual inflation:

$$\dot{\pi} = \lambda\left(\frac{\dot{P}}{P} - \pi\right)$$

This is, of course, simply an updated IS-LM model. Its short-run behavior can be represented by a two-panel diagram like figure A.1. On the left we represent the determination of the real exchange rate (in terms of the local-currency value of foreign exchange, *FX*), and on the right the determination of income; the *IS* curve shown there includes the effect of the interest rate on the real exchange rate and hence on net exports. From an initial equilibrium like point E, a fiscal expansion would move us to a point like E', raising income while appreciating the currency; a monetary expansion would move us to a point like E'', depreciating the currency.

In practice, even advocates of the Mass. Ave. model have in mind something a little more complicated, which takes into account the effects of lags in the adjustment of the trade balance to the exchange rate. The effects of such lags on the adjustment process are discussed in appendix B.

Appendix B
Financing and Adjustment

This study, like the conference on which it is based, has focused the bulk of its attention on the process of trade adjustment per se, and not on the macroeconomic background to that adjustment. Along with the controversies already discussed, however, the conference addressed two related questions about the context in which the decline of the dollar and of the US current account deficit have taken place. First, how is it possible for the US current account deficit to have declined so much when its supposed twin, the federal budget deficit, is headed for record highs? Second, why was the United States able to continue attracting foreign funds from 1985 to 1988 in spite of declining US interest rates?

Although a full treatment of these issues is a subject for another study, this appendix sketches out some answers.

The End of the Twin Deficit Era

The solution to the puzzle of why the budget deficit and the trade deficit have ceased to be twins is, like so many of the puzzles in recent US trade performance, a matter of details. For a variety of reasons, the numbers are not what they seem:

■ A large part of the recent increase in the budget deficit consists of the cost of the savings and loan bailout. This cost, however, is best understood as the explicit recognition of a hidden government liability rather than as a new expenditure; depositors in thrifts are only being given money they thought they had in any case. Thus, the cost of the thrift bailout does not reduce national saving.

55

■ For analytical purposes the remainder of the deficit needs to be corrected for both economic growth and inflation; as a share of GNP the deficit maintained a steady downward trend from 1985 to 1989.

■ The 1990–91 recession has worsened the actual deficit, but not the full-employment deficit (i.e., the deficit that current policies would generate if productive factors in the United States were fully utilized).

■ Finally, what matters for the current account is national saving as a whole, not just the federal component, and there has been some revival of saving in the private sector.

In a way it was a fluke that for much of the 1980s the uncorrected budget and trade deficits tracked one another as closely as they did. One would normally expect there to be enough nuisance factors complicating the picture to make the two deficits look quite different; we are now living in such normal times.

Financing the Deficit

A deeper conceptual issue is the question of how the United States was able to continue to attract capital inflows in spite of falling US interest rates in the second half of the 1980s. As pointed out earlier, this ability to continue financing the current account deficit until a low dollar could bring the deficit down was crucial to the United States' ability to avoid a hard landing. Was this success just a matter of luck, or was there a more fundamental mechanism at work? Without attempting a full accounting for US (and foreign) macroeconomic developments from 1985 to 1990, we can sketch out a stylized version of the adjustment process as it actually occurred; from this sketch it is possible to see that the ability of the United States to attract continued capital inflows was not an accident.

Imagine a country described by the formal model of appendix A, with the crucial addition of substantial lags in the response of the trade balance to the exchange rate. (A formal treatment is given below.) Suppose that this country combines a fiscal contraction with a monetary expansion just large enough to leave output unchanged. We have already seen that in the medium run this policy change will lead to a lower domestic interest rate; the lower interest rate will induce a currency depreciation; and the currency depreciation will lead to a fall in the current account deficit.

In the short run, however, currency depreciation will not reduce the current account deficit; rather, because of the J-curve, it will normally actually raise the deficit. Unless investors are willing to continue financing the deficit, the currency will fall without limit; yet the interest rate foreign investors are offered has fallen rather than risen. What keeps the capital flowing?

The answer is that the fall in the currency itself generates the necessary incentive. Suppose that investors were in fact unwilling to continue financing the country's current account deficit following a change in the policy mix. Then the country's currency would have to drop to a very low level to bring the current account into immediate balance, but it would recover from that low level once trade flows had had time to respond. Such a fall in the currency followed by a predictable recovery, however, would offer international investors the opportunity for large capital gains if they were to buy the currency during its period of weakness. These prospective capital gains would attract capital inflows—and these inflows would themselves limit the actual fall in the exchange rate. So, unless there is some additional reason for a collapse of capital inflows—for example, the fear of debt repudiation—capital inflows will be available to finance a transitional current account deficit following a policy change, even if that policy change lowers the domestic interest rate.

The actual extent of the currency decline is determined by the incentives required by investors. Following the policy change, the currency must fall to a level *below* its expected value in the medium run; this perceived undervaluation leads investors to expect it to *rise* in the future.[1] The size of the expected appreciation must be enough to offset the lower domestic interest rate, and thus assure the country of contin-

---

1. Or, more strictly, the expected rate of appreciation must be greater, or the expected rate of depreciation less, than the expectation before the policy change.

ued financing. Or, to put it another way, in the short run the currency must fall to a level that makes domestic assets look like good buys to international investors; the perceived cheapness of domestic assets is what attracts the financing needed to bridge the transition to a lower external deficit.

To see this more formally, consider a slightly modified version of the model of appendix A, in which trade adjusts to the exchange rate with a lag. A simple way to build such a lag into the algebra was suggested by Dornbusch (1976). We suppose that the *volumes* of exports and imports depend, not on the current real exchange rate, but on a "permanent" real exchange rate that is some distributed lag on past exchange rates. Net exports then depend both on this permanent exchange rate and on the actual spot exchange rate, with the spot exchange rate actually having a perverse effect because depreciation raises the relative price of imports. So we have:

$$NX = NX(Y,Y^*,R,R^P)$$

where R^P is the permanent exchange rate. We suppose for simplicity that R^P simply adjusts gradually toward the current spot rate:

$$d(R^P)/dt = \lambda\ (R-R^P)$$

The process of adjustment can now be described in terms of figure B.1, which plots R^P against R. For any given monetary and fiscal policies, a higher value of R^P will have a contractionary effect on the economy, because it will lower net exports; this will lower the interest rate and lead to a lower valuation of the currency. Thus, the relationship between R^P and R at any given point in time is described by the downward-sloping curve XX. Also, at any point in time the permanent exchange rate is given; but over time this rate tends toward equality with the actual exchange rate, so that medium-run equilibrium lies on the dotted 45–degree line.

Suppose that the economy is initially in equilibrium at point A, and that there is a shift toward a contractionary fiscal policy offset by monetary expansion. At any given level of R^P this will imply a lower interest rate and therefore a lower value of R; thus, XX shifts down to

FIGURE   B.1   Temporary undervaluation and financing during adjustment

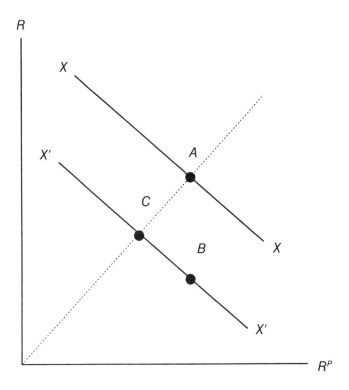

$X'X'$, with an eventual equilibrium at C. In the short run, however, the permanent exchange rate is predetermined. So the economy initially moves from A to B. At point B the current account deficit is actually larger than at A, because of the J-curve. Over time, however, as R^P adjusts, the economy will move from B to C; as it does, the current account deficit will be steadily shrinking. Rising net exports will also tend to pull up the domestic interest rate; hence, as we can see from the figure, the currency will be appreciating. It is the expectation of this appreciation that makes investors willing to finance the initially larger and slowly falling current account deficit.

This formulation is of course far too simplified and mechanical to capture the reality of the actual adjustment process after 1985. In particular, the behavior of the exchange rate is neither as predictable nor, in general, as rational as the model assumes. Nonetheless, this story helps to show how financing and adjustment are related, and why international markets will usually be willing to finance an adjusting country through the J-curve.

References

Baldwin, Richard. 1988. "Hysteresis in Import Prices: The Beachhead Effect." *American Economic Review* 78:773–85.

Baldwin, Richard, and Paul R. Krugman. 1989. "Persistent Trade Effects of Large Exchange Rate Shocks." *Quarterly Journal of Economics* 104, no. 4 (November): 635–54.

Bryant, Ralph C., Gerald Holtham, and Peter Hooper, eds. 1988b. *External Deficits and the Dollar: The Pit and the Pendulum*. Washington: Brookings Institution.

Bryant, Ralph C., Dale Henderson, Gerald Holtham, Peter Hooper, and Steven Symansky, eds. 1988a. *Macroeconomics for Interdependent Economies*. Washington: Brookings Institution.

Cooper, Richard N. 1971. "The Nexus Among Foreign Trade, Investment, and Balance-of-Payments Adjustment." In Commission on International Trade and Investment Policy, *United States International Economic Policy in an Interdependent World*. Washington: Government Printing Office.

Cripps, F., and W. Godley. 1976. "A Formal Analysis of the Cambridge Economic Policy Group Model." *Economica* 43:335–48.

Cripps, F., and W. Godley. 1978. "Control of Imports as a Means to Full Employment and the Expansion of World Trade." *Cambridge Journal of Economics* 2:327–34.

Dornbusch, Rudiger. 1976. "Exchange Rate Expectations and Monetary Policy." *Journal of International Economics* 6:231–44.

Dornbusch, Rudiger. 1987. "Exchange Rates and Prices." *American Economic Review* 77:93–106.

Dornbusch, Rudiger. 1989. "Give Japan a Target and Say 'Import'!" *New York Times*.

Dornbusch, Rudiger, Stanley Fischer, and Paul Samuelson. 1977. "Comparative Advantage, Trade, and Payments in a Ricardian Model with a Continuum of Goods." *American Economic Review* 67:823–39.

Economic Report of the President. 1984. Washington: Government Printing Office.

Fallows, James. 1989. *More Like Us—Making America Great Again*. Boston: Houghton-Mifflin.

Feldstein, Martin. 1985. "American Economic Policy and the World Economy." *Foreign Affairs* 63, no. 5 (Summer):995–1008.

Fetherston, M.J., and W. Godley. 1978. "New Cambridge Macroeconomics and Global Monetarism." In K. Brunner and A. Meltzer, eds., *Public Policies in Open Economies*. *Carnegie Rochester Conference Series on Public Policy* 9. Amsterdam: North-Holland.

Frankel, Jeffrey. 1988. "Ambiguous Policy Multipliers in Theory and in Empirical Models." In Ralph C. Bryant, D.W. Henderson, G. Holtham, P. Hooper, and S. Symansky, eds., *Macroeconomics for Interdependent Economies*. Washington: Brookings Institution.

Godley, W. 1979. "Britain's Chronic Recession—Can Anything Be Done?" In Wilfred Beckerman, ed., *Slow Growth in Britain*. Oxford: Clarendon.

Goldstein, Morris, and Moshin S. Khan. 1985. "Income and Price Effects in Foreign Trade." In R. Jones and Peter B. Kenen, eds., *Handbook of International Economics*. Amsterdam: North-Holland.

Helkie, William L., and Peter Hooper. 1988. "The U.S. External Deficit in the 1980s." In Ralph C. Bryant, Dale Henderson, Gerald Holtham, Peter Hooper, and Steven Symansky, eds. *Macroeconomics for Interdependent Economies*. Washington: Brookings Institution.

Houthakker, Hendrik S., and S.P. Magee. 1969. "Income and Price Elasticities in World Trade." *Review of Economics and Statistics* 51:111–25.

Johnson, Harry. 1958. "Toward a General Theory of the Balance of Payments." In *International Trade and Economic Growth: Studies in Pure Theory*. London: George Allen and Unwin.

Kuttner, Robert. 1991. *The End of Laissez-Faire*. New York: Knopf.

Lawrence, Robert Z. 1990. "US Current Account Adjustment: An Appraisal." *Brookings Papers on Economic Activity* 2:343–82.

Marris, Stephen. 1987. *Deficits and the Dollar: The World Economy at Risk*, revised ed. POLICY ANALYSES IN INTERNATIONAL ECONOMICS. 14 Washington: Institute for International Economics.

Marston, Richard C. 1989. "Pricing to Market in Japanese Manufacturing." *NBER Working Paper* 2905. Cambridge, MA: National Bureau of Economic Research (March).

Marston, Richard C. 1990. "Price Behavior in Japanese and US Manufacturing." Philadelphia: Wharton School (mimeographed).

McKinnon, Ronald I. 1963. "Optimum Currency Areas." *American Economic Review* 53:717–24.

McKinnon, Ronald I. 1984. *An International Standard for Monetary Stabilization*. POLICY ANALYSES IN INTERNATIONAL ECONOMICS 8. Washington: Institute for International Economics.

Mundell, Robert A. 1989. "The Global Adjustment System." *Rivista di Politica Economica* (December):351–466.

Prestowitz, Clyde V., Jr. 1988. *Trading Places: How We Are Giving Our Future to Japan and How to Reclaim It*. New York: Basic Books.

US Congress. House. Committee on Foreign Affairs. Subcommittee on International Economic Policy and Trade. 1981. *U.S. International Economic Influence: Agenda for the Future*. 97th Cong., 1st. sess., 1—25 (24 February).

Whalley, John. 1985. *Trade Liberalization Among Major World Areas*. Cambridge: MIT Press.

Williamson, John. 1985. *The Exchange Rate System*, 2nd ed. POLICY ANALYSES IN INTERNATIONAL ECONOMICS 5. Washington: Institute for International Economics.

Other Publications from the
Institute for International Economics

POLICY ANALYSES IN INTERNATIONAL ECONOMICS Series

1 The Lending Policies of the International Monetary Fund
   John Williamson/*August 1982*
                          ISBN paper 0-88132-000-5   72 pp.

2 "Reciprocity": A New Approach to World Trade Policy?
   William R. Cline/*September 1982*
                          ISBN paper 0-88132-001-3   41 pp.

3 Trade Policy in the 1980s
   C. Fred Bergsten and William R. Cline/*November 1982*
   (out of print)   ISBN paper 0-88132-002-1   84 pp.
   Partially reproduced in the book *Trade Policy in the 1980s*.

4 International Debt and the Stability of the World Economy
   William R. Cline/*September 1983*
                          ISBN paper 0-88132-010-2   134 pp.

5 The Exchange Rate System
   John Williamson/*September 1983, rev. June 1985*
   (out of print)   ISBN paper 0-88132-034-X   61 pp.

6 Economic Sanctions in Support of Foreign Policy Goals
   Gary Clyde Hufbauer and Jeffrey J. Schott/*October 1983*
                          ISBN paper 0-88132-014-5   109 pp.

7 A New SDR Allocation?
   John Williamson/*March 1984*
                          ISBN paper 0-88132-028-5   61 pp.

8 An International Standard for Monetary Stabilization
   Ronald I. McKinnon/*March 1984*
   (out of print)   ISBN paper 0-88132-018-8   108 pp.

9 The Yen/Dollar Agreement: Liberalizing Japanese Capital Markets
   Jeffrey A. Frankel/*December 1984*
                          ISBN paper 0-88132-035-8   86 pp.

10 Bank Lending to Developing Countries: The Policy Alternatives
    C. Fred Bergsten, William R. Cline, and John Williamson/*April 1985*
                          ISBN paper 0-88132-032-3   221 pp.

11 Trading for Growth: The Next Round of Trade Negotiations
    Gary Clyde Hufbauer and Jeffrey J. Schott/*September 1985*
                          ISBN paper 0-88132-033-1   109 pp.

12 Financial Intermediation Beyond the Debt Crisis
    Donald R. Lessard and John Williamson/*September 1985*
                          ISBN paper 0-88132-021-8   130 pp.

13 The United States–Japan Economic Problem
    C. Fred Bergsten and William R. Cline/*October 1985, rev. January 1987*
                          ISBN paper 0-88132-060-9   180 pp.

14 Deficits and the Dollar: The World Economy at Risk
    Stephen Marris/*December 1985, rev. November 1987*
                          ISBN paper 0-88132-067-6   415 pp.

BOOKS

FORTHCOMING

A World Savings Shortage?
Paul R. Krugman

Sizing Up U.S. Export Disincentives
J. David Richardson

The Globalization of Industry and National Economic Policies
C. Fred Bergsten and Edward M. Graham

Trading for the Environment
John Whalley

The Effects of Foreign-Exchange Intervention
Kathryn Dominguez and Jeffrey A. Frankel

The Future of the World Trading System
John Whalley

Adjusting to Volatile Energy Prices
Philip K. Verleger, Jr.

National Security and the World Economy
Ellen L. Frost

The United States as a Debtor Country
C. Fred Bergsten and Shafiqul Islam

International Monetary Policymaking in the United States, Germany, and Japan
C. Randall Henning

The Economic Consequences of Soviet Disintegration
John Williamson

Reciprocity and Retaliation: An Evaluation of Tough Trade Policies
Thomas O. Bayard and Kimberly Ann Elliott